<<terrain grammar>>

Jane Joritz-Nakagawa

<<terrain grammar>>

by Jane Joritz-Nakagawa

ISBN-13: 978-0-9883891-9-9

Acknowledgments: Work herein has thus far appeared, in some cases in earlier versions, in the journals *Cordite*, *Delirious Hem*, *FourW*, *New American Writing*, *Otoliths*, *Tokyo Poetry Journal*, *Truck*, *Upstairs at Duroc*, and *Zoomoozophone Review* as well as the chapbook *diurnal* published by Grey Book Press and the ebook *terra form(a)* published by The Argotist Online.

I'd also like to acknowledge that I drew upon artwork of Nakamura Hiroshi （中村宏） when composing a part of this book ("slow pull").

Notes: The language used in <a test of poetry> was taken from Charles Bernstein's poem "A Test of Poetry"; a couple of phrases in "demifugue" came from the kindle book "affective disorders and the writing life."

Cover Art: *Spinning in Space 3b* by Marcus Grandon © 2018 Marcus Grandon

Cover Design: Wendy Glaess
Typesetting: Andrew Maxwell Sixberry Tills

Thanks to everyone especially Steve Tills.

theenk Books
107 Washington Street
Palmyra, New York 14522
To order: http://theenkBooks.com
Contact: theenkbooks@twc.com

Also distributed by Small Press Distribution
1341 Seventh StreetBerkeley, CA 94710
http://www.spdbooks.org

Also by Jane Joritz-Nakagawa

Poetry:

Skin Museum, Avant Books, 2006
Aquiline, Printed Matter Books, 2007
EXHIBIT C, Ahadada, 2008
The Meditations, Otoliths, 2009
incidental music, BlazeVOX [books], 2010
notational, Otoliths, 2011
flux of measure, quarter after press, 2012
season of flux, quarter after press, 2013
FLUX, BlazeVOX [books], 2013
Wild Black Lake, Hank's Original Loose Gravel Press, 2014
Distant Landscapes, theenk Books, 2015
diurnal, Grey Book Press, 2016
Poems: New & Selected, Isobar Press, 2018

E-books:

Invisible City, White Sky, 2012
terra form(a), The Argotist Online, 2017

As Editor:

Women: Poetry: Migration, theenk Books, 2018

Contents:

i fold into myself
in my hermit kingdom
eating plankton everyday
entryways blocked
protocols stolen
a range of items
mispronounced
like the teeth of a saw

remedy advance
omniscient pavement

sickly uniform
exchange headstone

thump cyclone
adulterate unit

fleetingly diagnostic
especially fracking

whenever ancestor
buck room

secrete muscle
generation stains

distance basket
bouncing courtesy

proxy hernia
rainbow cursor

faux radio
welt crash

warring fractions
upholstery elite

special synthesis
favorite contempt

classic stranger
sorting award

plastic hallway
troubled fume

smoking typology
album drone

conclusive cards
laughing privilege

unexpressive net
diced memory

window justice
handheld sigh

irrelevant hazard
uninterrupted sleeve

indelicate pool
enjambed vista

vintage prong
non-normative feeling

(stuck in impossible buildings)

dizzy elegance
in a binary diagram

the bedsheet wind
is deafening

imaginary portraits in
sedated reflection

brittle flags for
vinegary excuses

pulse friendly a
buffed environment

scripted bodies
boycott levers

oversized facial
for bandaged perfume

casual stooges
lift up slime

sentimental abandonment
of polite zeroes

platform veneer
wears methane dress

voices never reach
stripped of private lives
data drones lie under digital clouds
rules of professional conduct under surveillance

hegemony in poetry
for ancient spying
we kiss in black and white
on days stars died

a wilted room clings to a small bird
(there is little room for animals)
alone in a meeting a chair barks
like a mother with infinite patience

leaping over wooden barn doors
old paper becomes romantic dark and clingy
dormitories don't speak aloud when
drowning cats are worn visibly

an angry frustrated island goes to
the front of the line
we had no choice but to do something
in defense of future sewage

freeing me from further blame
submerged shadows not afraid
to scale mountains
fractured sentences provide a framework for disaster

and the lamp remains downcast

A winking river
looks straight into a camera
while adopted pets launch ad campaigns
to surf with birth parents

searching inside a book a fountain
screams out: give me rhubarb!
truth drips out of pictures on the wall
until all that's lefty is soggy unwashed

certificates proving we are still
unborn nothing depends on
slow movements of clocks
manufactured hastily in previous centuries

*　　　*　　　*

pieces of dust are agony
when it's all violent and smeared as up
goes the lazy arm of a sofa you wade
against as if wheelchairs

were dim starlight meant for
aimless scratching to last year's failed musical revues
but i love the nook of you as a
basement opt out, in case

i fall from space while becoming fond of
burnt out moons moving me to cheers
armed robbery is a sandwich
too small for certain planting

flowers gaze sullenly

at a distance

*   *   *

human toy in a magnetic soundtrack
cataract air underneath is
affection is death.
sudden geometry in a muzzled river

let delusions harden you, please
plump my leaderless life!
my asian bookshelf is seaweed
all night long motel

for daisy muscles me
continually until my head
is stuck upright in
the trembling morning

*   *   *

four simultaneous
walls move toward
me but i evade it
with surplice coffee   a

wordless sky (s)trapped
in folklore calligraphy
a simple crush on ejaculation
on my face a searing

poem simulating my
anatomy

The surface is always
the program.

* * *

Endlessly objects collide
wandering divinity
as immense surplus
of whistling fields

Some people talk
too much and watch
too much TV
The cursor may be

her only friend
I think your pants
are silly, the cushion is too big
in dreams where all the parts

are randomly labeled
To quicken you
To ballast
some of my best friends are

tableware / on trains
squeamish computers conspire
with relentless rhetorical devices
my space is blank,

a soap opera of language surrounds me
i long for your body so much
that i wear a helmet
at all times

like a dressmaker
stripping language of
all its power and influence
i used to think about you

until i stopped
(i reminded myself to hate you so living
alone would be bearable. i could
turn my feelings on and off

except when i couldn't)
At a distance
a clock glares at me
At a distance

my tear falls
on a mountain
in a lost photograph

*   *   *

Released from your voodoo
arm, enmeshed with
mausoleum measures
of sky,

I could not distinguish my
thoughts from the alphabet
in the blemished world
of my minds

In morally bankrupt
versions
ballast is bereft
i hope you captive,

salty pirate,
wherever the ship sails

a chaos of pointless acts and exploding emotions
its sorrow in a swamp

love is a faulty device
protecting me from prayer
a grander silence creates a gullible apocalypse in
the form of a poem pressing
itself into my forehead

like a happily entrenched urn
a self that is not mine
loose hairs away from the body

expansive landscape, mesh of melting
into the foreground
lightless world (words)
twilight wor(l)d
beyond words, naked rain

vivid reconstructions of wor(l)ds
language, or something like it
clarity is unavoidable

a view from nowhere of an impending
disaster in a world preceding language
language as a loss (of wholeness)
an outside world continues independently

explanations come close to an end
in another part of the mind

internal and external worlds (wounds/words)
an analogue of mo(u)rning

i am a gun

a sentence goes one way, me another
a conversation begins ends or continues

i stand before no horizon
the earth isn't earth
maybe it's linoleum

i am thinking of the sex lives of snails
of misshapen flesh and swollen legs

a refuge of chains
my back is a disaster

my whiteness
the face of the government there

beefing up the rank
stench magnetic tape of culture
universal smoldering
sojourn poetic
of forthcoming ambience
of future ambivalence

always in a strange city

reduced to mind
representation of figure

signal of memory
compressing names

gesture of boundary
rupture in circle

how undergone accident
underdog resemblance

constitutes a center
mobilizing plentitude

future as enclosure
informs pure spending

duration of phenomena
succession of remainders

eroded rhythm sleeps
failure of constellation

dwelling in perception
by means of errant systems

precipice of heaven
old as prey

shifting of existence
stranded in longing

split by desire
secretion of homestead

voyage of canvas
imposes spandex

playbook distant
unborn rhyme

unsung chaos
recent ice storm

adjacent to fantasy
construction of starlight

dialogue breathless
contagion rocky

preordained tumult
performing seduction

gripping of ceiling
issues of suspension

identity of closed
empty of wailing

purchase of history
tree-lined fable

shudder of street
intersection of objects

the song's breathing
in a hierarchy of sentences
an ash of preludes

in the midst of sliding territories
infectious dust

my understanding of this moment
gone forever

under the fern
half of bone

color and shape
a dark sea

the final gazing
out of a birdcage

the old complaints
are the best complaints

slow pull towards silence
shifting frames of reference
i'd do anything to be alone
dark corridor

dreamy landscapes with flowing boundaries
messy undulations in my head
dying from invisible wounds
silent and distant

guided by reasoning
perfect sounds emitted, evaporate
at the edge of the alphabet
glimpse of expatriate emotion

next to a sullen cross
meandering on dulled skin
fixated on school uniforms
blades of interior

moving past quivering darkness
eye in the forest
colliding wooden park bench
not even a raised skirt

to match an eyebrow
wilted flower code
assault upon language
both sides of a coin

yellow and black
false dilemma on an empty train
images faster than an eye
palm trees in a row of sorrow

no one speaks
of bark of sunlight
a man whimpers at the clouds
somewhere a young girl

plastic flowers in a pink bedroom
my back crooked from watching
yellow barges in pushing away sense
in a portable landscape

stars trapped in nets
dire thrown carelessly
diced food
dark web of buildings

in a summer heat of reason
split open like a moving variegated shadow
across a black canvas
are pink lines

weblike forest
yellowed lips of sense
against a moving
target of glitter trees

thoughts leftover
soundless atmosphere
slow move away from fading language
to which i pin my hope

great blur of reason
new versions of radiant forests
at the deaf of feeling
a hundred views of 富士山

outdated throng of tired listening
dissolve into grey pools of regret
yellow objects in my mind
not this heavy lifting of concrete

enigmatic grave in the text
walk ending in madness
lopsided form of balance
dispensing reason

sleeping on damaged flowers
we walked all night
in the city where he was beating her
lack of symmetry

planets line up
for easy handling
thrust deep within
my stale vagina

torn streets and bent houses
in a fragile past
terraced cemetery
permitting no passage

bundle of sticks
hurriedly on the surface
sterile bed of consoling trees
words belonging to the earth

wreckage of human existence
innermost doll
yellow tulips
against a black fence

words of leaves
lopsided bag of weeds
mirror text
floral scission

shrub of memory
in the failing arms of another other
dull shard of language
pierces me

incomprehensible stammering of trees
impossible dialogue
rubble of words
rips floral utterance to foreground

hesitant walk on the moor
historic encounters with large feet
inaccessible impoverished language
leading away from homelands

川
川
川
川
川
森木林石水火雲霧
incoherent forest struck by
metaphysical lightning

beloved murders
shrines without temples
linguistic bodies
never recovered

fatal homage
between theory and a world
however i think
a tomb of poetry

gilded ether feminine shadow
hygiene of fabric
scientific chemise

chokepoint anew
scanty chemistry
torque scheme

ethnic frill / icy
balloon / unforgiving
intimate shocks

without a scalp
crossroads of dying
sing the domestic

inanimate velvet
holler their niche
glory now tongue

paradise body
exotic misfit veil
bleeds telltale pillow

partial fingerprint
animal trophy
adverse event

distinguished academy
my measurements
a form of adultery

states of becoming
when i am thru w/u
incompletely demolished

the same empty
disapora routine
blood bath

leaves in my bed
leaves unconscious
head wounds

flame color reaction
escorts superficial
rampant flamboyance

movement of branches
wants to chain
the hidden landscape

entrance to canyon
blow flat dimension
massive sky flits w/velocity
drained of desire gauzy weed
colonial trigger raw noise awry

environs of entangled
sequence of craft safety
smelting pot of couture
let me be language
in all its stupidity

museum season in leaky aisle
stands in the sitting room
abstract laundry hides
surreal apronry
gap of distilled edges

royal drudge near loose
animal downfall
chiseled weaponry fluted out
vulgar in its peak
of pure display

bone sandwich
garter freeze frame stands on ceremony
intrusive garland distributed
an effect of language
manifold smoothing

raging quench stuck with magic sprinkles
matching brutality perseveres ever
calendar grip sprouts prayer
if ever a far moth dotes
on window dressing dark blank safety magnifying

footsoles of yesterday's tragedy
here's hoping
redeemed nest of air
pneumatic community leans sullenly against
ominous inputting device

in the messianic metropolis of seduction
puzzling like private space
languishing in gene pools
forever spurning death tolls likely to rise to the occasion
every crude gesture awaits

lesbian in my head
useless consciousness bailouts
forgive my father who has sinned
in logical testaments to paralysis
a view of rotten flowers

in an imagined landscape
applied to language
sprout wings where defenseless
pouring all day
to the right and left of meaning

toward the peripheral
harbinger of ethics
displaced by language
a notched grammar
mist forced into words

a tightening.   an anger.   the rope and the whip.   the sinking
and the grinding.   the swallowing. a filthy bed.   a panic.

the covers, opened.   a body alongside.   a wet hand.   a strange feeling.
vomiting.   other kinds of secretions.   unfamiliar sensations.   not moving.
not speaking.   a blank sound. a hollow.   something filling it.   running
toward a door. a door moving further and further away.   your body against.
wood grain.   a panic.   a decision to keep smiling.   A decision . . . .

protect birds with thread like hands on top
a Noh chant sounding like hand hitting cans is wordy
press down with hands on bent persons
wings differ
naked from peeling off clothes like fruit
gauze like thread of a bird's net

thunderous rain on a field
rely on head to request a bundle
disconnect each entwined thread
dairy produce in each wine jar
wanton supervision of flooding water
railings of eastern wooden gates

an official holds a box
diarrhea after cutting rice for profit
to wear on the feet are corpses' footwear
separate bird from the lidded box full of odd insects
a willow tree above a horse's bit
a dragon stands on a simple electric current

a grain of standing rice
prosper in life while sitting cross-legged on the peak of a high hill
sulfur is a rock that flows without water
capturing a tiger using Mars
and further thoughts about tigers
understanding a child may need arms to feel complete

cool water capsized
hunting dogs use odd shaped claws
imperial tombs on hills near upturned feet coming out of the ground
to go toward or away on big and little days
is a way to cure sickness

provisions of rice in the village one day
a tiny amount is the value of the village below the cliff
principles may align people neatly
while neighbors meet nightly at wells adjoining hills to eat rice
tears and returning water
accumulate threads in a field

a fort built on four earthen fields
you may strive to climb 10,000 cliffs
but return to a big door
and a bell of metal rung by kneeling people
zero rainfall ordered today
the spirits line up in the rain

a slave is seated and shown to the samurai
age is determined by ordering a count of teeth
beautiful hoofprints of deer
atop calendar of days under a roof and trees
inferior due to little strength
a fierce row of fires
and clothes cut to bone

{because i speak only one language (with you)
ongoing struggle w/}

[falling in
your mist]

convulsed body of night
praises the murderer

& guards the end of hope
becoming a woman toiling in a factory

open sallow mouth to accept withered words
forces of chaos make a nightmare of love

continuing to resist mountains
placed upside down by demons

who prefer to live in thresholds
of lost wombs largely confined to the deep

random speech controls
my buoyancy and depth

one goal being to find sites untouched by men
while swimming slowly along a gelatinous floor

and no one pronouncing my name correctly
which looks completely ragged: rocks

without their faces
aesthetically limited due to their

preoccupation with sociology (that pseudoscience!)
all the while promoting the dominant culture's

mainstream values: a culture that has arisen around this
ideal represented indiscriminately as violent

criminals -- love relationships are just
not that important (however one feels)

about it -- a form of dependence was always
there, signifiers with no referents

-- to some people this appears to be a limitation

(not looking at me when i talk to you
the violin is a difficult instrument

that speaks loudly and slowly with exaggerated gestures
for a homecoming with no home

like a living fossil in a barren environment in which
few survive)

grotesque restlessness of recovery amplified
by temporary promises, a carefully worded bed, tantrum
after our fling of bling. Your beloved turbulent
voice of escape. A predatory building lost in
dwindling twilight

In a once innocent landscape, whining while meditating,
an asian apocalypse flowers into an inexhaustible
body mural, after centuries of naked ache, lessons
in unreal silence. Ruled by ordinary horizons,

thanks very much, foreplay for embossed massages
scrawled on the backs of the overworked and disfigured,
a master of invalidation, improved weaponry, *my little country*
speaking to me from behind a wall

. . . face of a samurai on a sofa cushion. A holistic mode of thought labeled
madness. The tiny space I'm allowed, garments which prevent action. My
mouth falls between my thighs and screams.

Logic of the swamp. Dark, troubled past stripped of meaning. A
self-oppressing mother. Living cadaver in chaotic topology.
Blood-stained persons.

Quasi cause, certain bonds (or not). Limited returns. Antidote to intimacy.
Lost cities. Collective amnesia. The weight of decay on my tongue.

Deleted and swollen. Words go where they want. On a small patch of land.
A pulsation swallowed by multiple horizons.

serenade of every awful angel
painstaking bootstrap fantasies

isolate fracture
captured in increments

belonging to belongings
accumulation of isolation

the inside of elaborate
vacuum of relationships

plowed fields like brooding children
does the contents of barricade

hereditary courtesy
readdress my feet

my eyes go far
reflective of my social class

what windows feel like
is what money looks like

syringes attached to all maps
rifle regions of unwarranted meaning

thirst of painted blossoms
at my majesty's pleasure

points always taken
hidden in refuse

gestures thick with disaster
syntactic malfeasance

immigration disaster
faulty celebrity magnet

in the midst of dreams
that don't happen

in vanished surface
dimples of language

my heart is plain
it's someone's fault

resurrection of infamy
in fingers of language

fractured hope stamped with auroras
joints of language hiding in melancholy trees

veins of language
produce translucent bindings

steady decline of sea
never known in obtuse pantomime

bring me the defunct perfume
of vacant eyes

embroidered with morbid gullibility
feminine souvenir of macabre

dancing silverware
in profuse certainty

morsel of bewilderment
evaporates treatise of moon

behung with wigs
classless symphony

blessed monster of mercenary
divides obscure momentary relief

replaying oncoming glottis
seductive adornment

animal suns
preferred as perfect charms

chiffon dragons of escape
open my veins

(over) the impoverished lands
(of) my body

(a) bony canvas of bent
trees overgrown (with) spindly bushes (beside(s))

(lodged) in the dim building where my heart (lies)
pale, pale legs where my head (is)

(a) living inkblot
planted . . . in place (of)

where does the poem go
(a) fuzzy remorse

(in) the burrowed furnace that consumes my ===

you only die once
with all the fairies at your bedside

whipped piper of love!
downy theorem where

every1 gathers at the hem
of blistering waterfall

to always be be/side
one (my/your/her)self

in your telescopic arm(ament)[s]
leaves consume my/a body

(a) worm enters (me)
(my) toes, now greying, begin to branch (toward)

those suffering severe repression may feel alien (to themselves)
we do not notice things in broad daylight if (they are not there)

and thus die toward/of a language. as it may [have been]. turning (in that
direction). whirling verb (of) personage. not grasped (to). in

search of [nautical roughage like as]. to displace (to). at refuse (of)
historical bending past. expands breadth toward/beyond

urchin of noun objects. forgetting of it now. (a) breach of always.

planted ... in place of . . . japanese scream[s] . . . whimper
dreams which were somewhat elder[ly] follow the waving branches

and is night
is always night

three narrow buildings
incandescent with rage

unrepaired bridge
falls into a concrete-walled stream

perpetually scratching the surface
my lost country

scraps of language
inside myself a lost child waving

thin fabric
in perpetual heat

the high seas
assume a wrongful place at a throne

swallowed by green land
distracted by faint traces of lack

wind composing obituaries for silent birds
i feel a blade

of grass on my neck blue
flowers sprout from fissures in my skin

(what type of flower does not matter)

talking points of
sprawling space

becomes faint(er and fainter)
with tiring [h]ands

to feel young again in a different field
with money which grew narrower

breathing fast, his soft waist
gradual accidents befall

swatting at the darkness pretending
we are strangers

the truth of appearances
fading monthly, ending reluctantly

(unnecessary surfaces are always masterpieces)

at 45 degree angles
bent over the table, more furniture

vile and hypnotic
soothing me like nothing else

bodily harm and strips of dull silver
in the word "prescription"

how long will my spirit
end badly

half a person equals political malaise
lost in an interior life

absentee poets objectify myself
erasing the cityscape

ghost ship in brackish water
wayward thought

phenomenological corset
pollution and contagion

hesitation wound
shoot fish in a barrel

engulfed cities between day and night
example of silence

fallen world [intermittent in my landscape]
identify with cliffs

punching down loaves of reason
proffered as tombs

defunct song and memory
in the lifelessness of a poem

shape the sun
death with another person

apprenticeship to myself
rigor and decomp

transactions between language
induce me to spawn

always surround me
not a walk in the park

invasive species
eyes turning inward

of their own volition
trying to enter the language

migrant crisis
days too long

who messed up the story line
embedded in wrongdoing

how long will my spirit be broken
residual dew of you

checkpoint disaster
although i'm dying my persona's thriving

une phrase traverse la tete endormie:
レジ袋有料化、過半☒が☒成

A is a child adult trapped in an aging body, protected by every1
B thinks everything is some1 else's fault
C imagines failure as the result of all her actions, thus seldom acts
D can't be alone
E is a loner since the death of her mangy cat
F thinks his children are objects for his amusement pleasure & gratification. he confuses thus their good performance w/love.
G as a child took care of her parents and now as an adult takes care of every1 but herself
H cuts herself
I is bulimic
J can't look people in the eye
K is jealous of every1 including the unlucky ill poor and depressed
L faces job discrimination due to her disability
M is still in the closet
N still plays w/dolls
O masturbates all the time
P has an STD is ADHD and has PTSD
Q is a blank
R puts every1 to sleep
S is hypersensitive to her own needs while oblivious to every1 else's
T's rage petrifies me
U makes holes in the walls of his house w/his feet
V is bipolar with a unipolar dog
W is a paranoid schizophrenic with handguns hidden all over the house
X burned down his house when he got bored with it
Y has sex w/his stepdaughter
Z fails all tests of reality

D-J=U
V+W-H=Z
N divided by (I+Q) = E
Y+B=T

parked outside
as ominous
lonely
 isolated ... there
drained objects
 chlorine smell
-- on its way

behind trees
back from the ground
        where the world
goes on like traffic
fixated
 impossible to
more than
  once

where the -- go silent -- its excess
                 violence is
       raising its head
makeshift
                 flittering down
       as it builds
                    oncoming
          nowhere
has
already   happened
this much
   attachment
collapse   invisibl(y)

too humid
an abstract phase
and visible
working with machines
via thresholds and samples
imagined differently
rhizomatic
multi-channel
unsewered
gritty asphalt
drive right through
perhaps they mean
making it impossible
village houses

hang listlessly

symbol of heaven
good train with well-equipped commodities
piece of land

hide of an animal
who or what has stalled
insignias of air

uncle hodgepodge
placed in buckets
metaphor for a river

test of poetry
lading carried
under his skin

camphor trees
agitate lightly
rashes of ash

harbor of illusion
slumberous friend
made of wood

its enclosing surface
if the floors
nominate candidates

curved, crooked or bent
farm which you imagined
structure in general

hunting game
in the ordinary sense
boats with thick bottoms

witless witness
reverence, yield, submit
metallic sounding instruments

drop down wounded
as of the mind
you can always xerox it

social assembly
a kind of trousers
eccentric passageways

one who fakes
see it all gray
overall mesh

for remote possibilities of escape

a person in pain exceeds language

inventing herself and watching herself [die]

i cannot recall events

as what happens is what feels untrue

& belongs nowhere & walks endlessly

if nothing tangible is at stake

mornings in bed, mostly alone

into this disfigurement

conversing with corpses

mumbling beside

mimesis of unfathomed archetypes

as a rigid joint

at the bottom of a wastebasket

each word its own planet

haunting the body

merging of potential shapes

in elusive pools

during a test run

that would become a life

biofuel or stage symbol

what becomes undone or lurks beneath

my frozen heart her upturned body

a set of relations

(has no language)

moving images

audible, lie in wait

my heart in italics again

glance through me

your hand and its shadow

faraway snow

breathes

in your mouth

forgotten letters

singed with grief

if not for

the finest of feeling

covered in silence

another eye behind an eye

talking to a wall

rapid edge

branches in brown bundles twisted with rope

create a fence

around an anonymous house

darkening

a forest grows thick around us

as indented song

erases the skin

leaving only grey bone

i place my foot at the entrance

to the house and wait there

in a corner of a park

a child with blonde hair

her parents are gone

(I never asked for these eyes, this skin)

under the same heavy thatched roof

look, let's talk about the future

so close it's gone

fading flower the air is crisp face in a mirror

sudden light trudging through the forest cicada on its back

youthful memories bicycles racing by filth on concrete with yellow leaves

a dead insect lands on my vagina footprints lost in deep snow joyful trend

crocheted sky

strange quiet sunlight

rustle of curtains moving

flooded street

worlds which scream

Advent of
Beguiled
Cacophony for
Dictaphone
Extemporate (exterminate)
Foreign in
Guileless
Hidden
Ideals
Just when you thought you
Knew what
Lies ahead
Most of it is
Not going to happen
Overall
Penpersonship
Questionnaire to
Review
Suck
T**
Unveiled
Veracity
Whoops
Xrays
Your
Zebrahead

Winning soul custody
Each and every
Absent flower
Stellar alphabet
Acerbic impersonation ~
Straightjacket sayonara

To know we're not alone in the world

          true day of feeling

In a monochrome sky

                    perpetual witness to myself

in the language of dreams

                    heaps of trash

leading to this now

disappearing into hope   re-entering despair

in flashes of misperception

                    every day i die for that meadow

NOTES
"sun" refers to "headlock"
"kindness" is rice stuck to a ceramic white and blue bowl
"I" is a fumigated tatami mat on which mangoes sit
"itadakimasu" is slang for poached fish
"tatami" is a battle scar
"op cit" is a disease-carrying mosquito dangerous to pregnant women
"highlands" is an alias for anonymous people
"for my flowering husband" was written by an unknown author who wishes to remain anonymous
"to remain anonymous" refers to poetry in general

no longer responding to painful stimuli

(no longer responding)

under my fingernails

copy of my neck

do not wake the body

---

the world is only this failure

my body of words

discarded by hope

floating empty on the surface of language

why anyone would jump what language does not reveal

receiving messages just often enough

to remain in a state of confusion

beyond the window

wherever you look

multiplicity of sameness

watching the village uselessly

I was not invited

That night, every night

(some must have cancer)

orange-studded sky

in a heavy-lidded room

village without a soul

(some have no escape)

worthless instrument

spoiled food

my tongue swells

on the tip of a photograph

in the direction of a ruined country

I enter into a dialogue

of myself,
a syllable of me

anonymous and ambivalent

the knot is tied
I did not invent the lock

To never be alone
in the mountains
a barren land of figures

leave the fragments be, do not try
to put them together. It's better
not to recall the entire nightmare

a wind carrying your smell
never reaches me
in a frozen wilderness

tantalizing distance
is anther form of
togetherness and
forgetfulness of the world

--

Raised not to trust
myself I don't know if the
cloud is white or
green if I should go buy the
axe at the home center if axe
is the center of home if this brand
of detergent will lead to
unrest in another country (should i
go there too? If so when? Why? To
do what?) I can only move
if you move but you're not

--

nerve ending
never ending or
beginning
in pursuit of
space
absent minded objects
fill the space
for final resting places
may agony be lovely
in place of objects

in praise of objects

endless ways
of defeating the stars

interior landscapes for
internal objects

world containing
families disappeared long ago
something is missing . . . .

too tired
to feel

content with words
instead of things

fragile envelope of skin
exceeding the ego's capacity for regulation

Last night I dreamed Tom Cruise plus a less attractive unknown white male actor helped me build a spaceship because I was unable to do it alone. And there was a deadline. It was like one of those American reality shows like Project Accessory where you have to make something by a deadline and then people judge your work, usually harshly of course. I know nothing about building spacecraft. It was very tense. So these guys especially Tom helped me. And I had this giant crush on Tom even though not in real life. I mean the actors I have had crushes on have been people like Terrence Howard and Toshiro Mifune. You know I moved to Japan hoping to meet and marry Mifune, who is however forty years older than me, or would be, if he hadn't died in 1997. But I always had a daddy complex. Anyway the spacecraft was also like a cannon. It didn't work too well so Tom had to physically hold me inside the cannon and then push me out with his arms throwing me into a crowd -- as I exited the cannon which was pink and sparkly and had a rifle attached to it that the other actor had his finger on the trigger on, i screamed lady gagagagagagagaga!! (because the cannon looked like something she would wear) and then I fell down into the crowd (Tom and the other actor went flying too, it was like an explosion like in the Mission Impossible movies) and it was like those dreams where you fly high above skyscrapers, except down below was what looked like the audience in the park for a recent Noh drama I saw except that few of the people were Japanese, it was more multi-ethnic. And unfortunately

somebody kept following us. And I lost my hat. Tom said Why don't you put this white towel (like the ones you get for free at Japanese onsens) on your head instead of that ugly hat, that's the ugliest hat I've ever seen, you look silly wearing it! And it's true. I have the hat on now and some of my neighbors actually run away, when they see me wearing it, it is scary to them. It really is an ugly hat.

I want my poems not to be experiences but representations of experiences by other people that they never should have had or would have been better off just imagining. I want poetry not to be mere objects but whirling dervishes of glory and hellbound ornamental sacrificial potential events of lustrous and lackluster illusory environments.

Words are not mere objects; they are also tools for really boring and trivial hallway conversations and stories that your friends pretend are intriguing for lying, instruments for governmental deception and capitalistic propaganda so that you buy things to ensure you are truly alive / but / and;of, So [what]

miscopied sky
wears forests on skin

points of exile
rape trial transcript

return the state pool
seedier part

blind violent sea
ceremonial autopsy

many things wrong
between blue and stutter

nothing is memory
bodies aligned

lime and rhyme
make up the difference

woody wind
transparent fleshes

northernmost heart
acrobatic cascades

silence lattice
symbolic porn

scarred door
facing torso

starry clothing
future colors

corridor feelings
diagram moon

frame of skin
lamp of hospital

on top of shaky wor(l)ds
barriers of doorsteps

everything in abundance
except epaulets

when you've walked on asphalt for too long
and chose being over doing

strange amounts of gravity
misshapen bladders

ready for battle
hedging my concierge

gradual shipwreck
blurred social propellants

books on naked body
unsafe water

offed the breeze and
slunk the albatross

slog the mineheads
graze the temple

further action required
on sloping mistress

rude barren of pinhead
pines for hailstones

denying wrongdoing
in treatment centers

strange depth of
accented pasture

imaginary languages
in fields of mysterious objects

hollow whirlwinds
misspent youths

neuro diversity
mythical blood

lost years power (of)
mystical attorneys

nonchalant flower
modesty panels

schematic evangelical
oblivious protocol

rejected as defective
disappointed horizons

exterior perimeters
enlarged data protection

heart --   in exasperated tones
heart, prologue
heart, murmur risen
any heart   harms the cycle form

turn round to unacceptable
urgency --   surfeit of lineage (chorus/coinage)
enter the immense feather of mood
-- to prison with the sky!

spheres of swirling bildungsroman
lie slinking with the moon
-- always lying

to commit treason against
the fluttering lawn filtered
with 007 mobilized under my
announced covers is

high damage -- present tense
high moon, future

熊

川　　　　　　　　　　家　　　　　　　　　　川 川
川　　　　　　　家 私 家　　　　　　川
川 鳥　　　　家 家 家　家

森森森
森

the day the bomb fell flash of sunlight my hair gleams in buckets

the day the police stop me
my arms flail upward
body warmed by sunlight on dead concrete

in unscented traces of habits
successful operation

pockmarked audience
inscribed on sound

incredulous drama
for display on mantlepieces

incomplete booty acquisition
stolen by mimics

insistent cemetery
provides fanfare for adjacent century

here is where my voice (trails off)
. . . . . （ドット）. . .

intolerable outskirt
interior stain

stalking on fake-book and insult-a-gram
please use a secure line

bludgeons the ancient
barefoot rescue team

bony thoughts
mouth of famine

scar of sun
crust of bone

rhapsody at midnight
your legal passport

splinters of tourist
nervous hissing

deep lines
sighted, chilled

scarce currents
claim the dense mountains

walking through shadows
mere fragments

foul arrival
upon bent stones

pungent passage
its hind legs

lots of relish
entering at its own risk

gently the streets darken
please cave in the day

eyes like wild birds
a deceased place follows me

deep silence under the weight
of thousands of abandoned wrinkled

leaves fountains of decay
permeate would be paradisal fault

lines of painful absence
for houses built on flimsy

excuses during fires
in detainment centers

scattered shudders in
mystical puddles become

bygone gardens leaking
from branches where

no one is talking amidst
bid rigging bed wetting and

acute organ failure
nonspecific threats

emanate from targeted
buildings where

no one is
listening or

inhabiting the space between
yet more objects

and there's crime
between my eyes

how to
continue

cold dew cries
because it's morning

cities are only
beautiful at night

in the daytime
i long for uninterrupted

rows of trees not
concrete buildings

with their laundry flapping
and grandpas smoking on

greying balconies
with metal railings

their wives sing insanely
afraid to go near the water

afraid of the weather
an artist is always being interviewed

i exit the back door unseen

a room full of poems
pinned to walls

poems emit from a wary
mouth

stiff immobile poems
fish tossed back into the sea

embraced by trees
i'm sitting there listening

but realizing i have little interest
in what is being said

this makes me feel
nauseous

i notice i cannot touch another human being today
so i put a pagoda next to a tea cup

to produce chaos out of order
a mask of divided dwellings

for future allotted thoughts
and youthful piles of insides

my impulse on the clock
lined in haze

a powder flame
around a glacial spirit

running to the moon
emitting oceans of script

mock vapor
of canine birth

in chalky fields
shrill signals loom across slopes

sunken trees, infinite blue
eaten mirror

nipples, direction, me, mother
scattered rush rods

bone nostrils rain replace heart citizens mobile

double bypass sampling program   contrast serum

unfeeling scrap of Jonas Kaufmann
too much of an impulse (impasse)   however poetry

to be somebody else   All the time
disorder   rises

straightens window

too early to tell
chorus of frowns

twerking a "decent" job
drifting from room to room

horrifically bored

she looks worse
than ever She

is a dog
she is my dog

grinning

twisting
languishing

teeming

tormenting/suffering
undulating

CENSORED
stealing

placating
blinking

obfuscating
sharpening

raping

decimating
decapitating

humiliating

misdirecting

torturing

thin armor of trees
free floating and detached

my flesh became a river

motif of debilitation
obsessive pattern

having no decorum
false starts and true endings

in the future of slaughterhouse animals

strict schedules of pointless tasks
uncontrollable motion of

shameful wreck
mental strata

lathering scars
words inflict damage

anonymous rocks
vigilante reunion

thankless rapids
je suis charlatan

political palette
chorus of frowns

aimless torture
good pair of bones

phantom disorder
tangential frontier

folklore of sky
canyon of mind

first tremor
entwined with touch

belly in the journey
maneuvers the wind

even the world
nothing follows

direction of the body
grass full of consolation

skin and sky
hidden in logic

stench of moon
uneven emblem

my soul's imaginary sight

runs aground with the speed of hope

chained to the roof

carrying out the same operations

system of time

with hollow doors

bricks piled up

in radiant sketches

assignment of centuries

resigned to monograms

perfumed law

stumbles across a bridge

drama of the street

empty hills, no one in sight

About the author:

Originally from the U.S., **Jane Joritz-Nakagawa** resides in central Japan. She is the author of over a dozen poetry books and chapbooks. She is also the editor of the theenk Books anthology *Women: Poetry: Migration.* Email is always welcome at the following address: janejoritznakagawa@gmail.com.

Also by theenk Books

Jennifer Bartlett, *Autobiography/Anti-Autobiography*, $12.95
Stephen Ellis, *OPULENCE*, $14.00
Steven Farmer, *glowball*, $14.00
Jim McCrary, *This HERE*, $14.00
Jane Joritz-Nakagawa, *Distant Landscapes*, $12.95
Aldon Nielsen, *YOU DIDN'T HEAR THIS FROM ME*, $12.95
John Roche, *Road Ghosts*, $14.00
Judith Roitman, *Roswell*, $12.95
Eric Selland, *Object States*, $12.95
Eileen Tabios, *The Awakening*, $16.00
Steve Tills, *Rugh Stuff*, $11.00
Steve Tills, *Behave*, $12.00

Anthologies

Women: Poetry: Migration, edited by Jane Joritz-Nakagawa, $25.00

Literary Journals

Black Spring, Issue 1, $7.00
Black Spring, Lawrence Issue, $7.00

Hank's Original Loose Gravel Chapbooks

Alan Casline, *The Cauldron Poems*
Crag Hill, *Yes James, Yes Joyce*
Alex Gildzen, *Percy and Bess*
jj hastain, *queer phylactery*
Tony Leuzzi, *40,000 Crows*
Jim McCrary, *Not Not*
Jim McCrary, *Po Doom*
A. L. Nielsen, *MANTIC SEMANTIC*
Judith Roitman, *Slackline*
Eric Selland, *Still Lifes*
Gerald Schwartz, *LVNG in TONGUES*
Steve Tills, *Invisible Diction*
Steve Tills, *Mr. Magoo*
Steve Tills, *Post Maiden*

www.ingramcontent.com/pod-product-compliance
Lightning Source LLC
Chambersburg PA
CBHW020702300426
44112CB00007B/474

* 9 7 8 0 9 8 8 3 8 9 1 9 9 *